My Mom, the Movie Star

Written by
Rob Waring and **Maurice Jamall**
(with contributions by **Julian Thomlinson**)

to act

limousine

to lie

movie

actress

movie star

famous

speech

joke

trick

In the story

Gemma

Kerry

Mr. Harris

Mr. Roberts

Mrs. Walsh

Anita

"Please find someone quickly. We need a speaker soon," said Mr. Roberts, the Bayview High principal.

He was speaking to Mr. Harris, one of the teachers at the school. The school Sports Day was the next week and they had to find someone to give a speech.

"Yes, I will. Sports Day is next week," he replied. "We should hurry."

Mr. Roberts said, "Good, but please hurry. And don't forget."

Mr. Harris's class was about American movies. Mr. Harris was very interested in old movies.

"There were many famous actors and actresses," he said. "The most famous were Judy Garland, Marilyn Monroe, and Anita Hamilton. Marilyn Monroe and Judy Garland died many years ago."

He showed them a picture of Anita Hamilton. "This is Anita Hamilton. She was very beautiful," he continued. "I'm sorry I only have an old picture of her. She used to be a great actress. She was famous for her acting."

One of the students, Gemma, quietly said to her friend Kerry, "My mother looks like Anita Hamilton."

Kerry and Gemma were talking. "Today is April Fool's Day. So what can we do to trick Mr. Harris?" asked Kerry.

Gemma said, "Here's an idea. Anita Hamilton looks a little like my Mom, right? And her family name was Hamilton before she got married, too."

"Yes, she does, a little," said Kerry. "So? What are you thinking?"

"Well, Mr. Harris doesn't know my Mom," said Gemma. "I'll tell Mr. Harris that my Mom was the famous Anita Hamilton. It'll be fun."

"That's a great idea. You're good at jokes," said Kerry. "Your mom used to be an actress when she was younger, didn't she? Her name's Anita, too, isn't it?"

"Yes, but my Mom's name is Anitta, not Anita," replied Gemma. "He'll never know if it's true or not. This will be really great."

When Kerry and Gemma were eating lunch, Mr. Harris walked in.

"Good!" said Gemma. "Here comes Mr. Harris. Let's tell our story, okay? Are you ready?" she asked quietly. "Do you know what to say?"

"Yeah, I'm ready," said Kerry. They talked loudly so Mr. Harris could hear.

"Gemma, I didn't know your mom was an actress," said Kerry.

"Yes, but it was a long time ago. She was in many movies," replied Gemma.

Mr. Harris heard them. He started to listen to them.

"Which movies was she in, Gemma?" asked Kerry.

"She was in *Love and Forever* and *Sooner or Later*," replied Gemma.

"When she was an actress, her name was Anitta Hamilton," said Gemma. Mr. Harris was listening very closely.

"Excuse me, Gemma," he said. "Did you say your mom is Anita Hamilton, the actress?"

"Well, umm . . . yes, I did, Mr. Harris," she said. "But that was a long time ago. Now she's Anitta Walsh."

"Really?" he said. "I saw all her movies. She used to be a great actress. Is she still making movies?"

"No, she stopped making movies a long time ago," said Gemma.

"I see," said Mr. Harris. "That's very interesting. Thank you." Mr. Harris walked out of the room. The girls laughed and laughed.

"Gemma, that was great!" said Kerry. "I really think he believes you!"

Mr. Harris went to see the principal. He said, "I found someone I can ask to give a speech on Sports Day."

"Great," replied the principal. "Who is it?"

Mr. Harris replied, "Anita Hamilton! She's the mother of one of the students in my class, Gemma Walsh."

"Wow!" said the principal. "She used to be a great actress. I really like her movies."

Mr. Harris said, "I can ask her to give a speech at Sports Day. Is that okay?"

"Sure. She'll be great!" said the principal.

MR. ROBERTS
PRINCIPAL

Later, Mr. Harris spoke to Gemma. "Gemma, would you please ask your mother to give a speech at school on Sports Day? Everybody would love to hear her speak."

Gemma was shocked. "Oh no," she thought. "But Mom wasn't that famous. She's not the real Anita Hamilton." Gemma's face went red. She did not reply.

Mr. Harris looked at Gemma's face. "Are you okay, Gemma?"

"Well . . . umm . . . yes, I'm okay," Gemma replied. She didn't know what to do. She was thinking. "If I tell Mr. Harris about the trick he'll be angry. If I tell Mom I lied about her being Anita Hamilton, *she'll* be angry with me, too. What should I do?"

Mr. Harris asked again, "Gemma, please ask your mother."

"Umm . . . okay," she replied.

"Thank you," he said.

Gemma spoke to Kerry. "Mr. Harris thinks that my mom is Anita Hamilton, but if Mom finds out our trick, I'll be in big trouble," said Gemma.

"Yeah, I know," said Kerry. "Here's an idea. Why don't you ask the real Anita Hamilton to come to the Sports Day?" asked Kerry.

"That's a great idea!" replied Gemma. "I'll call her now." Gemma found Anita Hamilton's phone number in the phone book. She called her.

"Hello, are you Anita Hamilton?" she asked.

"Yes, I'm Anita Hamilton. Who's calling?" Mrs. Hamilton asked.

"I'm Gemma Walsh from Bayview High School," she said. "We'd like you to come and give a speech at our school Sports Day next Saturday."

"Next Saturday?" she replied. "Oh, I'd love to, but, I'm sorry, I think I'm busy on that day."

Gemma was sad. "Oh, that's okay. Thank you. Goodbye," she said.

"Oh no!" she thought. "What am I going to do now?"

Later that day, Gemma came home. She didn't want to ask her mother about the Sports Day speech. But she didn't want Mr. Harris to be angry. "I need to ask her," she thought. "Maybe she'll say no."

She said to her mother, "Mom . . . ?"

"Yes, Gemma, what is it?" her mother asked.

"Well . . . umm . . . a long time ago, you used to be an actress, right?" she asked.

"Oh, yes! They were wonderful days. But I was never the main actress," she said. Her eyes opened and she dreamed of her acting days. "I really want to live those days again."

"Oh, no!" thought Gemma. "I can't ask her now. She'll say yes."

"Why Gemma?" her mother asked.

"Oh? Nothing," Gemma replied.

The next morning in school, Gemma was thinking what to do. "I'll tell Mr. Harris she said no."

Mr. Harris came up to Gemma and asked, "Hi, Gemma. Did you ask your mother?"

"Umm . . . yes," she lied. "She said she was sorry but she can't go."

"Oh? I see," replied Mr. Harris. "That's too bad!"

Gemma said, "I'm sorry, Mr. Harris." She was happy now. "I'm lucky," she thought. "Now Mr. Harris won't be angry, and Mom doesn't know. Everything's okay!"

"Thank you, Gemma," replied Mr. Harris.

"That's okay, Mr. Harris." Gemma smiled.

Gemma was at home. When she was doing her homework, the phone rang. Mrs. Walsh answered it.

"Hello," she said. "Anitta speaking."

"Umm . . . hello. I'm Joe Harris from Bayview High School," he said.

Mrs. Walsh said, "Oh, hello Mr. Harris. How can I help you?"

Gemma heard Mr. Harris's name. She was very shocked.

"Oh, no! Why's Mr. Harris calling Mom?" she thought.

Mr. Harris continued, "Mrs. Walsh, I'm calling to ask for your help."

"Yes, of course. How can I help?" she asked.

"I heard from Gemma that you used to be an actress. Is that right?" he asked.

Mrs. Walsh replied, "Yes, I did act in a few movies. But that was a long time ago. Why?"

Mr. Harris said, "You were my favorite actress."

"Oh? Thank you, Mr. Harris," she replied.

He said, "Would you please give a speech at school on Sports Day? Is that okay?"

"Well . . . umm . . . yes, it's okay," she replied. "I'd love to come."

"Thank you very much," said Mr. Harris. "A car will come and get you on Sports Day. Goodbye."

After the phone call, Gemma asked her mother nervously, "What did Mr. Harris want?"

"It was strange, really," her mother replied. "He knows I was an actress a long time ago. He asked me to give a speech at the Sports Day next week."

Gemma replied, "Oh, so what did you say?"

"Well, I said yes, of course," her mother answered. "I'm so happy. He still likes my movies and he remembers my acting."

Gemma was very worried. "Oh, no!" she thought. "This is terrible."

Later, Gemma was watching her mother. Her mother was looking at pictures of her acting days many years before. "Those were good times," said her mother. "It's so good that people remember me. It makes me feel good. I really want to be an actress again."

Gemma's face went red. She knew Mr. Harris thought her mother was Anita Hamilton. "I must tell her," she thought. "Anita Hamilton can't come so I must tell Mom that it was a joke."

Then she thought, "But Mom's so happy, I can't tell her now. Maybe it'll be okay on Sports Day."

On Sports Day, Mrs. Walsh started to get ready for her big day. Gemma was helping her. Gemma's mother put on some new clothes. She asked, "Do you think I look okay?" Gemma was very surprised. Her mother looked a lot like Anita Hamilton! She was very pleased. "Maybe Mr. Harris won't know she's not the real Anita Hamilton," she thought. "Mom," Gemma said. "You look great!"

Gemma looked out of the window. "Wow! Look at that limousine!" she said. There was a very big limousine waiting for Mrs. Walsh and Gemma.

Mrs. Walsh and Gemma arrived at Bayview High School in the big car. There were many people there. When Mrs. Walsh got out of the car, a woman saw her.

"Look. Anita's here!" she said, pointing. Everybody thought she was the real Anita Hamilton. Suddenly, everybody came to Mrs. Walsh. There were many cameras and many people.

Gemma saw all the people. She was very surprised. "Oh no!" she thought. "What are all these people doing here?" Her mother was surprised, too.

Gemma thought quickly and said quietly to her mother, "Mom, you can't go back now. You're smart. You're an actress, *be* an actress. You can do it!"

Her mother agreed. "Yes, I can do it. I didn't know so many people remembered me," she said quietly to Gemma.

The woman asked, "Excuse me, Anita. May I have a picture with you, please?"

"Of course!" said Gemma's mother. "Of course!"

Many people took pictures of Gemma's mother.

"Oh, she's so beautiful!" said one woman. Everybody was very happy.

Mr. Harris came to meet Mrs. Walsh.

Gemma said, "Mr. Harris, this is my mother. Mom, this is Mr. Harris."
Mr. Harris was very pleased to meet her. "I'm so pleased to meet
you. I'm Joe," he said.
"And I'm Anitta," Mrs. Walsh replied.
Mr. Harris said, "I love all your movies."
"Well, thank you so much," said Mrs. Walsh. "That was 25 years
ago. My face is different now. I'm much older."
"But you're still beautiful," said Mr. Harris. "And you are still my
favorite actress."
"Thank you, Joe," replied Mrs. Walsh. Her face turned a little red.

Mr. Harris said, "You should meet the school principal, Mr. Roberts. He's dying to meet you!"

"I'd love to meet him," she replied, smiling.

Mrs. Walsh met the school principal, Mr. Roberts, too. He was as pleased as Mr. Harris to meet her. Gemma and Kerry were watching them.

"Mom's doing a great job, isn't she?" asked Gemma.

"Yeah, she looks just like Anita Hamilton," replied Kerry. "We're very lucky. Everybody believes she's the real Anita Hamilton."

A woman from the radio station asked Mrs. Walsh, "Anita, may I ask you a few questions?"

Mrs. Walsh was surprised to see the woman. "Oh, umm . . . yes, of course."

The woman asked many questions. "What's your favorite movie? Are you still making movies? Who's your favorite actor?"

Mrs. Walsh answered all the questions. She really enjoyed the cameras and being famous. Gemma enjoyed watching her mother.

Later, Mrs. Walsh asked Gemma, "How am I doing?"

"Mom, you're doing great!" replied Gemma. "But I think it's time we went home."

"No, no. It's fun. I'm having a great time," her mother said.

Gemma saw Mr. Harris coming to them. She thought, "Oh, no. Here comes Mr. Harris."

He said to Mrs. Walsh, "Anita, we need you over here. Please come and give your speech."

"Oh no," thought Gemma. "The speech! Now everyone will know she's not the real Anita Hamilton."

Gemma's mother went on stage. Everybody was very happy to see her. She was a little nervous.

"And now . . . ," said Mr. Roberts. "The star of the day will make a speech." The people were very excited and very happy.

Then Mrs. Walsh saw the television cameras. They were all looking at her. She said to herself, "Wow, I didn't know so many people remembered me." She was very happy. She walked slowly up to the stage and spoke.

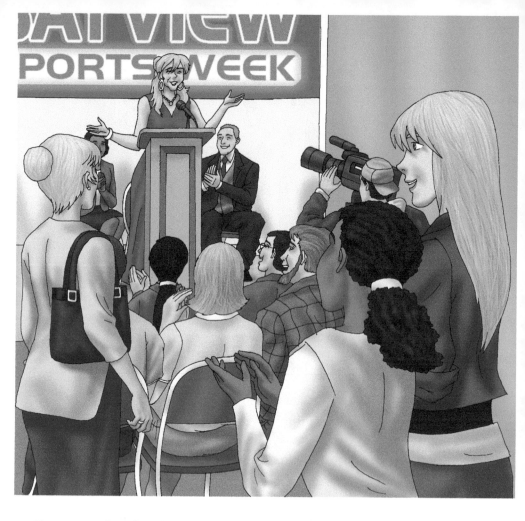

She started, "Thank you, everybody. I'm very happy to be here today . . . I'm Anitta." She spoke for a few minutes.

Everybody was happy to listen to her. Nobody was happier than Mr. Harris. "This is great," he thought. "I met Anita Hamilton! She's at my school!"

Gemma watched her mother give the speech on stage. "She's a really good actress," she thought.

An old woman was watching the speech. She came up to Mr. Harris.

The woman was the real Anita Hamilton! "Hello," she said. "I'm Anita Hamilton. A girl called Gemma Walsh asked me to come to the Sports Day to give a speech. I said I was busy, but I decided to come. Am I too late?"

Mr. Harris looked at her. He did not believe her. He thought Mrs. Walsh was the real Anita Hamilton! "She can't be Anita Hamilton!" he thought. "She's too old."

"I'm sorry, but Anita Hamilton is on stage. Please be quiet, she's speaking," said Mr. Harris.

"But I'm Anita Hamilton," she said again. "I don't know who that is on stage."

Mr. Harris did not want to talk to her. He looked at her and said, "I'm sorry, I'm busy now. Please talk to me later." He wanted to listen to Mrs. Walsh's speech.

Gemma and her mother went to talk to Mr. Harris. Then they saw the real Anita Hamilton talking to Mr. Harris. They were very shocked. Then Gemma's mother understood.

Gemma said, "Mom, the other day Mr. Harris called and he invited you to Sports Day, remember?" said Gemma. "Well . . . I told Mr. Harris that you were the famous Anita Hamilton. That's why he called you."

"What? So, he thinks I'm Anita Hamilton!" said her mother. "Why did you do that?"

Gemma replied, "Well, Kerry and I were playing a trick on him. It was April 1st, and it was a joke."

"Oh, I see," said her mother.

"Kerry said you look like Anita Hamilton, and your name is Anitta, too. So we thought it would be a good joke. But it wasn't," she said.

Mr. Harris and Mrs. Hamilton were very shocked, too. Mrs. Walsh spoke to the real Anita Hamilton. "I'm so sorry, Mrs. Hamilton. I didn't want to hurt anyone. Please don't be angry."

"That's okay. I don't like giving speeches," Mrs. Hamilton said.

Mr. Harris looked at Mrs. Walsh and Gemma. He was very angry. He said to Mrs. Walsh, "But, you're not . . ."

"No, Mr. Harris . . . ," said Gemma's mother slowly. "Gemma tricked you. She tricked me, too."

Mr. Harris looked at Gemma very angrily. "I'm listening, Gemma," he said.

Gemma told Mr. Harris and Mrs. Hamilton about the trick.

Gemma said sorry to Mr. Harris. "Mr. Harris, I'm really sorry. It was a joke. Kerry and I knew you liked Anita Hamilton, and we wanted to play a trick on you," she said. "I'm really sorry."
She continued, "I'm sorry, Mrs. Hamilton. I didn't want to hurt anyone. I told a lie and I didn't want anyone to be angry with me. It was all a big mistake."
Mr. Harris was very shocked. He said, "Well, Gemma. I think everybody needs to hear this story. Please go on stage and tell everybody what you did."
"Umm . . . okay, Mr. Harris," she said.

Gemma went on stage. Her mother and Anita Hamilton were there. She told everybody about the trick and about her mother and about the real Anita Hamilton.

"Everybody, I'm sorry," she said. "I played a trick on Mr. Harris, and this is not the real Anita Hamilton. It's my mother." Gemma's face was very red. Everybody was very surprised.

"But the real Anita Hamilton is here," she said, smiling and pointing at her.

Gemma and her mother walked home. "That was bad of you, wasn't it?" said Mrs. Walsh.

"Yeah, Mom. I'm sorry," said Gemma. "It was really bad."

Gemma and her mother thought about that day.

"But I did have a good time," said Gemma's mother.

"Yes, I could see," replied Gemma. "I thought you were a better actress than Anita Hamilton."

Gemma's mother smiled all the way home.